Contents

great self-esteem: what is it?

This first chapter will give you a good idea of where low self-esteem comes from, what maintains it and the consequences – and even benefits – of suffering from it. Very often poor self-esteem first develops during childhood and by adulthood has become a habitual way of thinking.

You will also make the acquaintance of your Personal Fault Finder (PFF), and will learn that it is your number-one enemy. You will begin to realize that your opinions about yourself may be historically learned and skewed, and that they do not necessarily provide a fair reflection of your self-worth.

Most importantly, you will grasp that self-acceptance is the way to kill low self-esteem stone dead and you'll start setting goals for yourself as you set out on your journey towards change.

What is self-esteem?

What do we mean when we talk about self-esteem? You will probably agree that it includes some, or all, of the following:

* the ability to enjoy life to the full
* the ability to cope with life's ups and downs
* feeling good about ourselves
* feeling that others, in general, like us
* having a positive attitude
* having good social skills
* the willingness to give new things a go
* the willingness to take risks
* the ability to make difficult decisions
* the ability to achieve life goals.

Self-esteem can best be described as having confidence in your own abilities and values. It does not mean thinking that you are the best at everything, but feeling comfortable with yourself even when you are not. It is accepting yourself, with all your strengths and weaknesses, while still taking opportunities for self-development.

In simple terms therefore, self-esteem means having trust and faith in yourself. Before you can do this, however, you need to like and value yourself. You also need to be able to accept yourself as you are. The 'catch 22' situation here is that, if your self-esteem is low, then these are tall orders.

Self-esteem is, in essence, a measurement. We rate ourselves against a variety of criteria, and the result is an estimate of our personal view of our value or worth. The problem is that we tend to rate ourselves very inaccurately and very harshly. This in turn leads to low self-esteem since, based on our negative perceptions, we continue to undervalue ourselves. Worse is to come – once a person believes something to be true, he or she will start to *act* as if it were. The person will start to gather evidence to support this erroneous belief, while at the same time discounting evidence that fails to support it, thus strengthening the negative view of his or her personal value.

Think about a time when you felt really confident – perhaps you had done something well, or someone had praised you.

* Did you need a particular achievement to give you this positive feeling?
* Can you remember having such a feeling without having excelled at anything special or receiving any particular positive input?

Childhood origins

Where does our low self-esteem come from? Are we born with it? Is it genetic? Do we learn it? Have life events simply conspired against us so that we feel everything we do goes wrong, and we never get that lucky 'break' that would give our confidence a boost?

Most people suffer from some element of low self-esteem. Problems usually develop when our self-esteem plummets so low that it starts preventing us from doing things: 'I'm not trying for the job promotion – I'll never get it anyway' or 'I didn't invite so-and-so to go out with me – they would be sure to say no, and then I'd feel even worse about myself'.

Where does this come from? Parents often feel that criticism encourages their child to be aware of their weaknesses and therefore try harder to improve.

So a child may learn that what they think is 'wrong' while what someone else (their parent) thinks is 'right'. For example: a father who says 'You idiot' when his son makes an error will scarcely recollect saying it, while the child absorbs the idea that he is an 'idiot'.

So, we can see how the low self-esteem habit can develop.

Can you begin to see how hard it is for any of us to grow up feeling particularly good about ourselves?

Adulthood: time to tackle low self-esteem

What we would like you to recognize is that the corrosive power of low self-esteem comes largely from external circumstances. This is natural.

A concept that will help you overcome this is self-acceptance. When you adopt the idea of self-acceptance, you begin to value yourself *in spite of what others think*. In the examples we gave you previously, low self-esteem has developed, in the main, due to the negative views and comments of significant others in our lives. If we can develop enough resilience to value ourselves in spite of what others may think, we will begin to feel much better about ourselves.

Exercise

Take one negative belief about yourself, for example: 'I'm hopeless at sport'. Next write down where this belief came from.

* What evidence do you have to support it? Write down at least three different pieces of evidence here.
* Now think about this for a while and then write down any evidence you may have to challenge this view. This can be as simple as, 'To be honest, I've never even tried football, so it is only an assumption that I would be useless at it.'

Don't worry if you find this difficult at this stage. You are simply learning to stretch your thinking at this point and to appreciate the difference between beliefs and hard facts.

Introducing your Personal Fault Finder

Low self-esteem prevents you from accepting yourself as a valuable human being. You can achieve a great deal by way of positive accomplishments in your life, and still suffer from low self-esteem. This is because there is a difference between an acceptance of your abilities on an intellectual level, and an acceptance of yourself on a personal level.

The architect of your low self-esteem is your Personal Fault Finder (PFF), whose job it is to constantly whisper in your ear, reminding you of your faults and weaknesses. Use your imagination to imagine what your PFF looks like. (Although this may sound childish, bear with us, it is actually a very helpful tool.) What about a pantomime character – tall and thin, in an ill-fitting suit and a huge top hat? Or a little gremlin that sits on your shoulder chattering away to you? You might even want to give your PFF a name. Using imagery in this way will help you to view your critical self as something (or someone) external to yourself that you don't need to keep listening to. In turn, it will be much easier for you to fight something you can visualize and whom you can tell to 'get lost' as your self-esteem improves.

Once bedded in, your PFF is very hard to dislodge. You learn to live with it and trust and believe what it says. One of the main goals of this book is to enable you to remove your PFF and see it for the fraud that it is. With a little work, this is quite achievable and you will be amazed at how differently you will view yourself without your PFF around to demoralize you.

Exercise

Conjure up a description of your Personal Fault Finder.
* Make it as colourful as you can. The more you bring imagery into play here, the easier it will be for you to deal with your inner critic. Make the caricature humorous, which will also be helpful.
* Now replay in your mind that last critical comment 'he' or 'she' made. Does imagining your PFF in this way help you to loosen the extent to which you believe the criticism?

Your PFF is a dangerous friend. Not only is it able to constantly remind you of perceived weaknesses, failures and inabilities – it also encourages you to believe that it is actually protecting you from harm. In turn, your self-esteem becomes even lower.

Your PFF encourages you to feel that avoiding rejection is better than experiencing it. The downside is, of course, that you fail to see that your negative predictions may have been wrong – you might have got the job or settled down with your lover.

Think about an area of your life where your confidence is low. What is your PFF telling you? What solutions does it come up with? How do these affect you? Does your self-esteem increase as a result of taking your PFF's advice? If not, why not? Doing this will increase your awareness of the way your PFF disguises its sabotage as 'help'.

The importance of risk taking

The saying 'To risk nothing is to risk everything' is very powerful. We must learn to assess risk, manage risk and take risk – or we will never move forward in life. It's beneficial to learn that there is no such thing as failure – there are only successes and learning experiences. It simply doesn't matter if we are not the best at everything or sometimes make mistakes. But your PFF won't let you see things this way. So it heightens your anxiety and fear of failing to the point that it seems quite unbearable for you to do so. Your PFF achieves this by running you down, then offering 'solutions' that appear to help but which, in fact, put the nail in your self-esteem coffin.

Your PFF is a false friend, and in the course of this book you will learn to silence it for ever.

Can you think of any examples in your own life where your fear of failure has prevented you from achievement? Looking back, how do you feel about that now? Now consider two or three times when you were very afraid, but undertook the task or faced the fear anyway. How did you feel afterwards if you gave it a go and failed? How did you feel afterwards if you succeeded? Which of these three feelings was the most positive? Which was the least positive? Why?

The consequences of low self-esteem

One of the saddest aspects of low self-esteem is that it tends to alienate us from others. Here are some common examples of how low self-esteem can affect how we think and behave. Notice any that you recognize in yourself.

It's everyone else

We tend to blame other people for our misfortunes: 'I would not have done this, if he had not said that.' We decide that we have been unfairly treated, without considering why. The more inadequate we feel, the more critical we become – it is as though finding fault with others helps us build ourselves up.

Pay attention to me!

Sufferers of low self-esteem rely on feed-in from others to make themselves feel good. They feel miffed and upset if this attention is not forthcoming.

Selfishness

Low self-esteem can breed selfishness. We become so self-absorbed, so wrapped up in our own needs and desires that we have little time to consider the needs and interests of others, even those we love and care for.

Coffee or tea?

We are so uncertain of our ability to make a good decision that we dither, procrastinate and become totally indecisive. This can lead to poor decision-making skills, which in turn reinforce the person's low self-esteem.

Poor me

We take on a 'victim mentality' and tell ourselves that we are the victims of circumstances that are outside our control. We believe it will make people feel sorry for us, and therefore pay us more attention.

Boastfulness

When we think we are inadequate compared to those around us, we may attempt to rectify this by trying to impress others and make them think more of us. In reality, we do ourselves a disservice and impress no one.

Over-competitiveness

Our need to be right all the time stems from a desperate need to prove ourselves to those around us.

These are just some of the ways that, in our attempts to increase our self-esteem, we end up lowering it even further. We have all been guilty of some of these things at one time or another. That is human nature. It is the *extent* to which we behave in these ways which can blight our lives. We need to learn to accept ourselves as being just fine as we are in order to get rid of these negative traits.

Exercise

Do you consider that any of the above traits apply to you? Be really honest.

Don't feel defensive about this – we all tend, from time to time, to attempt to boost our self-esteem using inappropriate tools. But it is very important to recognize what we do, and to acknowledge it, before we can start to correct it.

Introducing self-acceptance

Can you think of anyone you know who treats everyone else as an equal and usually speaks their mind? A person who appears confident but not arrogant? A person who seems to keep any mistakes that they make in perspective, who can listen or talk, work or relax, and seems constantly at ease?

You might say – if you have someone in mind – that this friend has high self-esteem or is very confident. Yet what we are actually describing here is a much more valuable commodity – that of self-acceptance. This person is one who accepts herself entirely as she is, and does not waste precious time worrying about what she is not. She does not constantly compare herself with others who do more, or beat herself up when she tries and fails, or makes mistakes.

Doesn't that sound a good way to be? Would you also like to be like that? You can learn how.

Exercise: testing your self-esteem levels

Even when we feel our self-esteem is very low, some of these negative feelings come from discounting our strengths and abilities, rather than not having any. Read and consider the statements below. Mark each statement on a scale of 0 to 4, according to the level you agree or disagree with it, where:

0 = never; 1 = agree occasionally; 2 = agree sometimes; 3 = agree most of the time; 4 = totally agree

When you've completed the test, add up your scores.

1 I consider myself to be a fairly worthwhile person.
2 I can take criticism reasonably well.
3 I don't take remarks people make too personally.
4 I attempt to encourage myself rather than criticize myself for my weaknesses.
5 When I make mistakes, I don't see myself as a total failure.
6 I expect most people to like me.
7 I am socially confident.
8 I make some contribution to society, even if only a small one.
9 It doesn't especially upset me if others disagree with my views.
10 While being aware of my shortcomings I actually quite like myself.
11 I feel that my life is fairly well on track.
12 I can usually deal positively with setbacks.
13 I attempt not to compare myself with others.
14 I have a sense of humour and can laugh at myself.
15 I generally consider that life is interesting and fun.

Score

A perfect 60
You *may* have a problem! Self-esteem that is too high can be as dysfunctional as self-esteem that is too low. Alternatively, wow, well done!

45–59

Why are you reading this book?! Of course, you can still gain useful insight.

30–44

You certainly need a boost, but you recognize some of your good points, so making positive adjustments should not be too difficult for you.

15–29

You are suffering unnecessarily from negative thinking about yourself. We hope that will have changed totally by the time you have worked through this book.

0–14

You have a very serious self-esteem problem. This book may be enough to help you, but if not, you might benefit from professional assistance.

Your personal view of yourself

We can be swinging along the road quite happily, feeling great, excited about the day ahead and then, guess what? We inadvertently catch sight of our reflection in a shop window. Suddenly we see that our hair looks a mess, our nose is too long; the general impression is just not great. The spring goes out of our step and we start ruminating about our lack of attractiveness. Our confidence drains away and the day doesn't seem so exciting and full of potential any more.

Does this sound familiar? Why do you think this happens? Your Personal Fault Finder is at work again.

The reason that it is so powerful is that it is hard at work all the time. Because it works all day every day, you become conditioned to believe this inner critic. Your PFF defines how you see yourself. Therefore you will only feel good about yourself if you can silence it or block it out somehow. This is possible up to a point. You may feel that you can prove it wrong by achieving something positive, for example losing weight or wearing a designer outfit that you know looks good. But these feel-good factors only last for so long.

This is because they are external factors. Your PFF is not in charge of 'externals'. It is in charge of your view of yourself.

Please ensure that you understand this very important point: your PFF ensures that you are *conditioned* to think negatively about yourself, which is why it is so hard to gain confidence and so very easy to lose it again. You won't defeat your PFF by constantly achieving external successes to countermand it, but by becoming so comfortable with yourself that it is rendered useless and disappears.

Think back over the last two weeks and a time when you felt really good about yourself. How long did that feeling last? Did any negative thoughts about yourself bring your mood back down again? Did you actually feel that it was more 'normal' to feel less confident in yourself? If so, you are stuck in a low self-esteem rut, and have been neatly placed there by your PFF.

Exercise: testing your personal view of yourself

Allow at least 15 minutes for this test.

First, make sure you have your notebook and pen to hand. We need you to time yourself as you do this test, so don't start until you have made a note of the start time. For the first part of this test, start now.
* List your top ten weaknesses or faults.
* Stop the clock! How long did that take you? Make a note.
* Now start the clock again, and complete the second part of the test.
* List your top ten qualities and strengths.
* Stop the clock again. Record your time taken.

What have you discovered? We suspect that you found the first part of the test much easier than the second part.

You may have been inundated with ideas for the first part of the test, yet were scratching about to find ten points for the second part. Your time record will show that you took a great deal longer to complete the second part of the test than the first.

What does this tell you? That you are a person with hundreds of faults and few good qualities? Or that your view of yourself is defined by a negative thinking style that you may actually be aware of, but feel unable to do anything about?

The second view is almost certainly going to be the real problem, but it actually doesn't matter whether you believe either the first or the second view.

All that matters is that you are comfortable with yourself – *however you are*. This is the core concept that you will learn as you work through this book. Once you begin to truly accept yourself, you will start to like yourself as well. Life is as good as your relationship with yourself.

Goal setting

It is important to set goals in order to achieve change. This may seem a strange suggestion after we have spent much of this chapter discussing the idea of being 'okay as you are' and accepting yourself, rather than relentlessly trying to change things.

However, feeling okay – and having good self-acceptance – does not mean that we give up on achieving goals; it simply means that we are still perfectly acceptable people if we don't achieve them, rather than useless duffers. These lines from Rudyard Kipling's famous poem 'If' illustrate this:

> *If you can meet with triumph and disaster, and treat these two impostors just the same. . .*

Good self-esteem isn't about winning all the time. It is about accepting yourself even when you lose.

There is also a difference between improving your *skills* and improving your *self*, which means learning to like yourself more.

Thinking less about improving your skills and more about improving your self – which may mean your perceptions of yourself – will help you to set worthwhile self-esteem goals.

Here is a question – well-known as the 'miracle question' – which makes goal setting much easier.

> *If we could promise you that when you wake up tomorrow you will no longer have low self-esteem, but will feel very confident about yourself, how would you know that this had happened? What changes would you notice in yourself (or in others) that would make it clear that our promise to you had been kept?*

Note down at least five things that would be immediately different for you. The answers should highlight your own personal goals. For example, if you wrote 'My boss would praise my contribution to the department a great deal more', then a personal goal might be:

* 'I would like to achieve more in my career' or
* 'I would like to have more confidence in the quality of the work I produce' or
* 'I would like to think of myself as successful in the workplace'.

If you wrote, 'I would receive more compliments about my looks', then a personal goal might be:

* 'I would like to feel better about my body image' or
* 'I would like to dress more attractively'.

Write down four major personal goals that you would like to achieve with improved self-esteem. Once you have achieved this, you will have mastered the skills to enable you to achieve all of your goals with less difficulty. This is because goal setting is about giving you a personal focus – something to aim for. In reality, the skills you will learn will be generic – that is, applicable in any situation, so you do not need to specify them all now.

The skills you will learn will enable your self-esteem to be robust and solid in all situations, not just those you have focused on.

unpacking your low self-esteem

In order to address your low self-esteem you have to start by understanding it – identifying and analysing exactly what the problem is for *you*. In this chapter we'll look at how low self-esteem is made up of layers of negative thoughts, assumptions and deep-seated beliefs that mutually reinforce one another and which together can have a deeply corrosive effect on the quality of our lives. But low self-esteem, we'll discover, is not just about negative thoughts and beliefs, it's about negative *feelings*; and it's this emotion that gives us our pain.

Crucially, though, our negative feelings are often not tied directly to the negative events themselves – a failed job interview, for example – but to *our own thought responses to them*. It's this mechanism that enables us to take control, to start tackling the way we think about the things that happen to us and ultimately to strike at the very heart of our low self-esteem. In this chapter we'll introduce what is likely to be the most powerful tool in your armoury – the 'thought record' – something we'll be returning to in later chapters.

Identifying the problem

Low self-esteem can be caused by a succession of failures, for which we blame ourselves, or a chronic 'drip, drip' of having been told throughout our childhoods that we're not up to much. Then as adults we look for evidence to confirm this idea and not disqualify it.

For some, it has been an all-pervading part of their lives for as long as they can remember. For others, good self-esteem was taken for granted, until an event – or series of events – changed all that. We work with many people who say: 'I used to feel fine about myself. Then that all changed...' They will usually identify:

* a time frame ('...two years ago')
* an event ('...when a relationship broke up')
* a period in their lives ('...when I went to university').

Take a moment to think about your view of your own low self-esteem. Is it generalized? Have you always felt this way – or can you point to a specific time, period or event in your life when you first lost your natural self-confidence?

The answer to this question will help you to identify whether your problem is unhelpful thinking or unhelpful beliefs.

Unhelpful thinking

This is where you have taken a negative view of events that have befallen you and incorporated these thoughts into your day-to-day thinking style. For example, you have always thought of yourself as attractive until someone you care for deeply ends a relationship, when you decide you must be unlovable.

Unhelpful beliefs

This is where our opinion of ourselves is defined by more absolute views – usually developed in childhood – which we consider to be facts. For example: 'I am a selfish person'; 'I cannot get on with others'; 'I'll never make a success of my life'.

Don't worry too much which you believe your problem to be – you may even think it is a mixture of the two. You will still be able to get rid of your Personal Fault Finder just as easily.

Consider where you feel your low self-esteem might come from, and what form it might take, for example: a response to a specific adverse event, or something you feel has simply always been there. Write down now what conclusion you came to.

* If you used to feel okay about yourself, what changed that?
* If you have always felt poorly about yourself, what beliefs do you actually have?

The examples we gave you on the previous page should help you.

The different levels of thinking

To learn how to feel good about yourself, you need to learn a little about the way your mind operates.

When you are feeling down and have doubts, people often tell you to 'think positively' and 'look on the bright side'. Do you sometimes feel like responding, 'Look, I would if I could'? Or do you sometimes agree – and actually attempt to do as you have been advised?

On the basis of this advice, we can simply say to ourselves, over and over 'I am *not* selfish' or 'I am *very* attractive' and our self-esteem should increase in relation to how often we repeat these mantras.

Why do you think this does not work? The answer lies in the fact that our thoughts won't hold any water if they are in direct contradiction to our basic beliefs about ourselves. These beliefs are not *necessarily* true (although they might be) but we *think* they are – which becomes the problem. You could have film star good looks, but if you believe 'I have a big nose that makes my face look ugly', then it really doesn't matter how many times you look in the mirror and repeat to yourself that you are good looking, you're wasting your time. You will never believe this mantra! So don't do that!

Beliefs versus facts

You need to begin to check out whether your beliefs are actually true. Do you really have a big nose, or is that what you see when you look in the mirror because someone at school once rudely suggested that you had?

Sometimes, our beliefs are right – in which case we can problem solve to make realistic changes. But challenging our beliefs – 'playing detective' to check their validity – is always the first port of call.

Exercise

* Do you ever attempt to 'think positively' when your mind is flooded with self-defeating negativity?
* Does it work for you?
* Consider when it makes a difference and when it doesn't.

When you have read to the end of this chapter, return to this point and see if you can give yourself a clearer explanation as to why this rarely works.

Negative thoughts, assumptions and beliefs

We have now mentioned negative thoughts, negative assumptions and negative beliefs. What is the difference between them? In defeating low self-esteem, it is important that you understand the relationship between them, as well as their differences.

Imagine your thought processes as being rather like a three-tier layer cake that would look a bit like this:

Day-to-day thoughts ('What an idiot I was to do that')
Assumptions (if this... then that...)
Basic beliefs (truths)

Negative thoughts are the 'top layer' of our thinking. They automatically pop in and out of our minds at the drop of a hat: 'Oh, I've messed up there'; 'I'll never get this right'. In fact, these thoughts are your PFF in full throttle! We call them negative automatic thoughts (NATs) because the moment something happens, there they are. No reasoning, no pondering or internal debating: purely and simply the first thought that comes into our head.

These NATs may be difficult to spot to start with, as you are so the first step is to learn to recognize them.

Just becoming aware of these thoughts can help you begin to think in a more helpful, constructive way and with time develop positive automatic thoughts (PATs).

Negative beliefs are the 'bottom layer' of our thinking. We regard them as absolute; in our minds, they are not open to debate, as we (often erroneously) believe them to be facts. We have negative beliefs about:

* ourselves ('I am worthless')
* others ('People always let you down')
* the world ('Crime is everywhere')
* the future ('Nothing will ever change').

Negative beliefs can be so deep that we rarely even consider or evaluate them. We see them as absolute truths – 'Just the way things are' – *but they are very often wrong*.

Usually developing in our childhood, when we may not question what we learn, these negative or core beliefs can keep us trapped in our vicious cycle of low self-esteem.

You need to learn to identify unhelpful beliefs that prevent you from thinking more positively about yourself and your abilities, and to learn how to replace them with more realistic beliefs that will stop holding you back.

Exercise

* Consider any negative or core beliefs you might have about yourself. Write them down. Use the explanations mentioned earlier to ensure that they are basic beliefs.
* Ask yourself, at this moment, how strongly you believe each of them on a scale of 1 to 10 (where 1 = not much and 10 = absolutely).

At the end of the book, you can re-rate them and see how much the strength of your beliefs has diminished.

Negative assumptions link our beliefs to our day-to-day thinking. In this sense, they are the 'middle layer' of our thinking. They also become our rules for living, for example: if you hold a negative belief that you are a boring person, then you may make an assumption that 'If I talk to people socially, they will find me dull and uninteresting'. 'I won't go to the party. No one will want to talk to me.' Or you may go, but decide 'I'll just stand by myself in the corner. That way, I won't have to talk to people.'

You may develop a rule for living, such as 'I should not socialize', as you consider this will prevent your 'I am boring' belief being put to the test.

Exercise

* Can you identify any rules for living of your own? Look back at any basic beliefs that you managed to identify.
* Now ask yourself how you cope with these beliefs on a day-to-day basis. For example, if you believe you are unlikable, your rule for living might be to be as nice as pie to everyone at all times to mitigate against this.
* Write down three rules for living that you tend to use to help you overcome some of your self-defeating beliefs.

The good news is that, as you gain in self-esteem and self-acceptance, you will be able to consign these rules to the waste bin.

The role of emotion in low self-esteem

Having negative thoughts isn't actually what upsets us. It's the *emotions* that such thoughts trigger that cause us pain and distress. If you think you are a 'born loser' but the feeling that this generates for you is calm acceptance, you will feel okay. If the feeling that this thought generates is total despair, then you will feel anything *but* okay.

Low self-esteem is problematic because it makes us *feel* badly about ourselves. Your thoughts generate these feelings. You *feel* the way you *think*.

Meet Peter. As he walks down a corridor to his office, he passes Jim. 'Hi Jim' says Peter, giving him a friendly wave. Jim walks on by and fails to acknowledge Peter at all.

If you were Peter, how would you feel?

* Depressed ('Jim obviously doesn't like me.')
* Angry ('How rude. He couldn't even be bothered to say hello.')
* Amused ('Silly idiot – he must have forgotten his glasses.')
* Concerned ('He was obviously very preoccupied. I wonder if everything is okay?')
* Equable ('Oh well. Jim isn't always over-friendly.')
* Disappointed ('He didn't notice my new outfit.')

To summarize: one event – two men passing in the corridor; five possible different thoughts about the event; five different feelings. . .

Why did we not finish the last sentence? Why did we not say 'Five different feelings about the event'?

Because the feelings were *not* generated by the event. The feelings were generated by the *thoughts* about the event.

Does this idea now make more sense to you? This is an exceedingly important point as it is the foundation upon which you will create good self-esteem. It means that, instead of having to change all your life circumstances, you can work on changing your thinking – a much less daunting prospect – and this will change the way you feel.

Practise 'unpacking' your thoughts and your feelings. Use the table in the following exercise. Look back over the last week and write down two or three events that have caused you to experience a reasonable level of emotion. Identify the emotion you felt and then write down what you were thinking at the time, or just before the event happened. Do you see more clearly how your thinking about the event largely determined how you felt about it?

Copy the table below. Fill in at least three lines today. Then fill in one each day for a week.

The emotion you felt	The event that triggered this emotion	What you thought when this happened (self-critical thoughts generated by your PFF)	(leave empty for the moment)
(e.g. anxiety)	(e.g. client forgot important meeting)	(e.g. he isn't taking this seriously; he probably feels I'm not good enough to do the work he wants done)	

Some people have trouble separating their thoughts and feelings. A simple tip is to remember that thoughts usually appear as sentences ('I hope I get this promotion') while feelings are almost always just one word: happy, sad, guilty, angry, cheerful, depressed, anxious, embarrassed and so on.

Bringing it all together – developing an understanding of the problem

Let's now bring all these thoughts, feelings and behaviours together, so that we can develop a shared understanding of what maintains someone's low self-esteem. Look at the following diagram, which offers one possible explanation of the effects of the negative thinking that can accompany low self-esteem.

As you can see from the following diagram (in CBT terms, known as a 'conceptualization' or 'formulation'), thoughts, feelings and behaviour are all linked. This linking is what *maintains the problem* and keeps our self-esteem low.

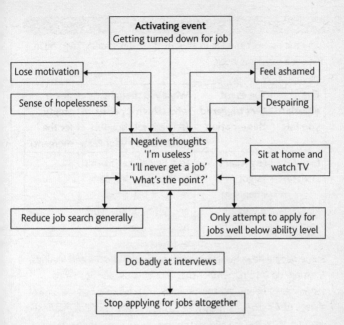

Negative conceptualization.

Now look closely at the arrows. They have two points, both outwards, and then back inwards. Each negative emotion and action that you have in response to your negative thinking feeds back to you to reinforce your conviction that your negative views were correct. In other words, the emotions and actions driven *by* the thinking *maintain* the thinking. Look again at this formulation – there is absolutely nothing here that is going to break this cycle of despair and hopelessness. It is feeding in on itself and nothing changes; the sad fact is that the negative thoughts that are causing all this may be quite untrue.

The good news is that we can tap into any one of these areas, make a few small changes, and those changes will have a knock-on effect on the other areas. The following diagram will show you this.

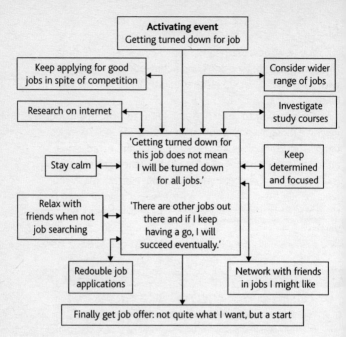

Positive conceptualization.

Can you see what is going on here? Look at the two formulations. The event was the same. Yet the event created thoughts which drove both emotional responses and actions that either maintained and consolidated the problem, or drove a way forward out of the problem. If you can appreciate and understand the importance of this, you will be well on the way to improving your own self-esteem immeasurably. Try it yourself.

Understanding where we may be going wrong is an essential first step, as is appreciating the basic relationship between thoughts, feelings, actions and outcomes. Now we need to move further forward and start to enable you to make the changes that will defeat your low self-esteem and replace it with a strong and healthily balanced view of yourself.

Using a thought record

You have now learned to identify your self-defeating thoughts, and the emotions and behaviour patterns that go with them. However, up to now, your PFF has had the upper hand.

The best way to challenge your PFF is to write down your negative thoughts and emotions, and then add more positive or realistic alternatives. This is called a thought record, since, although you are recording what has happened, the main focus is on what you *thought* about what happened. The more you practise filling in a thought record, the easier it becomes to spot these thoughts – and to understand the effect they have on how you feel.

Take a look at the thought record at the end of this chapter.

Exercise

Copy the thought record at the end of this chapter.
* Practise filling it in, working across the page.
* Fill in each column for at least one negative thought.

Don't worry if it does not come too easily yet. This is just a start.

Tips for filling in your thought record

Finding alternative responses

You may initially find it hard to come up with alternative responses. This is because your natural tendency is to be self-critical – and to believe these self-critical thoughts to be true.

Rating your thoughts and emotions

You will notice we ask you to rate (subjectively) how strongly you believe your negative thoughts, the intensity of your emotion, and the strength of your belief in the alternative responses. This is so that you can check that you have picked the thought that generates the emotion.

For example, if your negative thought is 'I am overdressed for this function' and your emotion is 80% panic, you may not have logged the right thought. Ask yourself *why* being overdressed is causing you such anxiety and you will get closer to your real concern. The answer might be 'I will look completely out of place and everyone will laugh at me.' *Now* you have identified the thought which might cause such panic.

This is an important point, as your thought record will not help you unless you are working with what really bothers you. So do take some time to consider what is *really* upsetting you.

Be firm!

Be very firm with your rebuttals; really challenge and talk back to your PFF. Come up with at least two or three alternatives. Find several different ways of looking at the same thing.

You may initially find that, although you come up with alternative thoughts, you don't really believe them. You still believe your self-critical thoughts more strongly as you have had years of self-indoctrination. This will gradually change – and you will learn further skills in later steps to help you to reinforce your beliefs in a more positive outlook.

Rating the strength of your emotions at the end of the thought record checks whether challenging the negative thoughts does in fact help you to feel better.

Once you are familiar with identifying negative thoughts, you can examine how unrealistic or unhelpful they are and whether they are useful to you.

Exercise

Begin using your thought record on a daily basis. Set yourself a goal of challenging one negative thought each day for the next two weeks. With practice you will eventually no longer need to write your thoughts down, but please ensure you do so initially.

A thought record

Date and time, and what happened	What you thought when this event happened (How strongly do you believe this on a scale from 1 to 10?)	How you felt (How strongly did you feel this on a scale from 1 to 10?)	Alternative thoughts (Generate at least two or three alternatives. Rate your belief in them on a scale from 1 to 10)	How do you feel now? (Rate any possible change, now you have looked at things more positively)

3

challenging your thinking and beliefs

Now that you are used to using a thought record – and used to the idea that you can improve your self-esteem – it is vital to challenge your existing ways of thinking and acting and to replace them with alternative ideas about yourself that will raise your spirits and make you feel a great deal more confident and accepting. We want to help you to develop a variety of skills and techniques in order to do this. A basic and simple thought record is a start – but only a start.

In this chapter you'll find confidence-building techniques such as 'ask a friend' and analytical aids such as the 'downward arrow' technique and the Positive Data Log. Sometimes these can seem like a lot of hard work, but, if you stick with it, you'll quickly discover that they are incredibly useful skills to acquire. Some will work better for you than others, of course, but try to think of them as different 'weapons' in your growing armoury as you take on your PFF.

Before we turn to these techniques, however, let's have a closer look at some typical distorted thought patterns.

Recognizing distorted thinking patterns

The feelings generated by low self-esteem such as depression and anxiety to name but a few, are caused by *distorted* thinking. Once you learn to challenge these thoughts, you will immediately change how you feel – both about yourself and life in general.

Recognizing distorted thinking is not always easy. We assume that all our thinking is rational and 'correct'. In a good frame of mind, it may be (though not always). But when we are in a poor frame of mind, our thinking can become negative and distorted without our realizing that this is happening.

The problem is that, once we start making thinking errors, we tend to 'stick with them'. They become assumptions and beliefs that we retain unless we make an effort to recognize and change them.

Psychologists have identified a number of common thinking errors that most of us make some of the time (and some of us make all of the time). If you know what these are, and recognize them, it will make your challenging rebuttals much easier to formulate. Place a tick against any you feel apply to you.

Generalizing the specific

You come to a *general* conclusion based on a *single* incident or piece of evidence. If you have a minor car accident, you decide you are a dangerous driver (and must never drive again). Someone treats you unfairly and you say, 'Nobody likes me'. You use words such as 'always' and 'never', 'nobody' and 'everyone' to make a general rule out of a specific situation.

When you challenge your thinking, ask yourself if you are taking a specific situation and making a general assumption about it. Be sure to turn this back to specific thinking. For example, if you make a mistake, don't tell yourself that you are hopeless, tell yourself that you did not do *that specific thing* as well as usual.

We all use distorted thinking patterns at times. With that thought
in mind, look at what you have already written in your thought
record.
* Have you made any generalizations about yourself or
  your behaviour?
* If so, create an alternative thought that is *specific*.

Mind reading

Mind reading is one of the commonest thinking errors we
make when our self-esteem is low. Without their saying so, we
'know' what people are thinking and why they act the way they
do. In particular, we are able to divine how people are feeling
towards us.
* 'I know he thinks I am boring.'
* 'I can tell she doesn't like me.'
* 'I'm sure they don't really want me in their group.'

Yet we are jumping to conclusions without any real
evidence – and, for some reason, we only seem to have the gift
of mind reading *negative* views.

Writing such thoughts down in a thought record will help you
to re-evaluate this supernatural thinking ability and challenge your
mind reading certainties.

Filtering

We take the negative details from a situation and then
magnify them, while at the same time filtering out all the positive
aspects, for example:

*You have dressed beautifully for a formal evening and your
partner pays you the well-deserved compliment of saying
how nice you look. However, as you leave the room he
mentions that the hem of your skirt is not quite straight.
You now feel that you no longer look lovely, and that the
evening will be spoiled. The fact that you look stunning quite
passes you by.*

Polarized thinking

We think of people, situations or events in extremes such as good or bad: 'I must be perfect or I am a failure.' There is no middle ground. The problem is that we usually find ourselves on the negative end of our polarized extremes. So if we cannot be perfect, we must be all bad. If we don't get the job we want, our future is ruined.

Catastrophizing

We expect disaster. We notice or hear about a problem, and start on the 'What ifs?', for example: 'What if tragedy strikes?' 'What if it happens to me?'

We then decide that if this terrible thing did happen to us, we would not be able to cope.

Personalization

This involves thinking that everything people do or say is some kind of reaction to us.

Perhaps your partner mentions that the home is looking a little untidy. You will immediately 'read' this comment as a criticism of your housekeeping skills.

You find yourself becoming unnecessarily defensive and possibly even causing ill-feeling if you take someone's passing remark as personal criticism.

Blaming

This is the opposite of personalization. We hold other people, organizations or even the universe responsible for our problems, for example:

* 'She has made me feel terrible.'
* 'That company ruined my life.'
* 'Life is so unfair.'

We feel unable to change our views or our circumstances, as we see ourselves as victims of other people's thoughtlessness and meanness.

It's all my fault

Instead of feeling a victim, we feel responsible for the pain and happiness of everyone around us. If your firm loses an important client, you will find a way to believe that something you did caused this.

Fallacy of fairness

We feel resentful because we think we know what's fair, but other people won't agree with us. We continually attempt to prove that our opinions and actions are correct. We expect other people to change their views and actions if we pressure or cajole them enough. We try to change people in this way when we believe our hopes for happiness depend entirely on their behaving differently.

Exercise

* Show the list of thinking errors from this chapter to friends, family and/or work colleagues, and ask them if they recognize any that they use themselves. (In all probability, they will smile wryly as they admit to most of them!)
* How do you feel, knowing that these are errors most of us make?
* Now look through your thought record and see if there is one thinking error that you use more than others.

Checking out possible thinking errors is another excellent skill to add to your toolbox. Make sure that you use it regularly.

More tools to help you challenge self-defeating thoughts

Checking for evidence

What goes through your mind when your challenge your PFF and write down more positive, rational alternatives? Many people write diligently, but the thought in their mind is, 'I don't really believe this – what I really still believe are the views of my PFF.'

How can you strengthen your belief in your alternative views? There is one extremely helpful tool – thought by many to be the most important 'thought shifter' around – and that is to ask a simple question: 'If this is really so, where's the evidence?'

Practise this skill. Look back to your most recent self-critical thought.

* Ask yourself what evidence you had to support it. If you were a barrister in a court of law, could you provide evidence against it? What would you say?

* Look at the full version of your thought record. You will see that there are now two extra columns. The first asks you to find evidence to support your PFF's negative comments. For example, if you have looked in the mirror just before going out and thought 'I look dreadful', where is your evidence? Is your hair a mess? (fix it). Are your clothes wrong? (change them).

* Start looking for the evidence to support your self-critical thoughts. You will usually find it harder than you think to come up with solid reasoning. Would the response 'Oh, I just do' stand up in a court of law? Would the judge accept it or throw it out?

* The second new column asks you to find evidence for your alternative thinking. Using the example from this exercise, an alternative thought might be, 'I really don't look too bad'. It will be easier to believe this if you write evidence that might be along the lines of:

  • 'My partner always tells me I look nice when I get dressed up.'

  • And/or 'My best friend has asked to borrow this dress next Saturday.'

* As you get used to finding evidence for your thinking, it will loosen your PFF's hold on your mind through tangible, logical argument, rather than simply repeating optimistic alternatives that you don't really feel hold water. This is a very powerful skill.

Full thought record

Date and time, and what happened	What you thought when this event happened (How strongly do you believe this on a scale from 1 to 10?)	How you felt (How strongly did you feel this on a scale from 1 to 10?)	Evidence to support your negative thought	Alternative thoughts (Generate at least two or three alternatives. Rate your belief in them from 1 to 10)	Evidence to support your alternative thoughts	How do you feel now? (Rate any possible change, now you have looked at things a little more positively)

Are you guilty of the tyranny of the 'shoulds'?

A great deal of negative, self-defeating thinking comes from using the words 'should', 'must' and 'ought'. These words imply personal failure almost every time we use them. They cause us to make demands on ourselves, and suggest that we cannot meet those demands, for example:

* 'I should have known better.'
* 'I shouldn't have done that.'

This is not positive thinking. We think this is positive self-talk – that we are motivating ourselves by telling ourselves these things. In fact, the exact opposite happens: 'I must be such and such (polite, charming, clever and so on)... and since I am not, I then feel badly about myself.'

And it's not only us. When our self-esteem is low, and we feel sorry for ourselves, these 'shoulds', 'musts' and 'oughts' extend to others. People 'should' be nicer to us. Others 'must' consider us when making their plans. Colleagues 'ought' to take into account how busy we are before dumping extra work on our desk.

We would like you to visualize yourself gathering all of these words up, and dropping them into the nearest rubbish bin.

What can you put in their place? One option is using acceptance; adopting the idea that it is okay to be fallible ourselves and that others also make mistakes.

Exercise

Focus on how often you use the word 'should', and replace it with a softer option. This will increase your awareness of this thinking error, and encourage you to make the change permanent.

Confidence-building technique: 'ask a friend'

Many of us have a tendency to be far harder on ourselves than on others. We make allowances for the mistakes of friends and work colleagues, we understand, for others, that a 'bad step' doesn't make a 'bad person' – yet when it comes to ourselves, we show no leniency.

An excellent tool for helping ourselves to be more self-accepting is this. Ask yourself the following question:

'If my best friend was feeling this way, rather than me, what would I say to them? What evidence would I point out to them to help them see that their pessimistic thoughts or negative self-assessment was not 100% true?'

The answer you will probably come up with will usually be quite different to your own, negative self-talk. We are always so much wiser and more constructive at finding positive qualities in others than we are in ourselves. Use your evidence-gathering skills to prove your point, and you will probably find how little evidence there is for the self-defeating thoughts that your 'friend' has.

Another good question to ask yourself is:

'Would my best friend agree with my negative views of myself? If not, what might they say about me?'

Most importantly, then ask yourself,

'Why would my friend see me differently to the way I see myself?'

Become your own 'best friend'. Use the questions above regularly, and you will find that it will really help to see yourself and your situation in a more positive way.

Exercise

* Jot down three negative aspects of yourself, or events where you feel that you did not come up to scratch.
* Now imagine that your best friend is describing these worries to you. Write down exactly what you would tell them.
* Does this give you a new perspective on your views about yourself?

Tackling negative beliefs

You may find it hard to move away from pessimistic thinking if your negative beliefs are deeply entrenched. However, you can still learn to replace these beliefs with a more compassionate and positive view of yourself.

Remember that while our day-to-day self-critical thoughts tend to evolve due to specific events, beliefs we hold about ourselves are absolute. For example: 'I am boring', 'I am hopeless' or 'I am unlikable'.

Can you identify any beliefs you may have about yourself that contribute to your low self-esteem? If you found that difficult, try this: think back to early experiences that encouraged you to think badly about yourself. What conclusions did you come to about yourself based on events in your childhood?

Think about the things you may do to keep yourself 'safe', for example: 'I don't socialize much'. Why not? Your answer may help you to discover a belief, for example: 'I am boring' or 'I can't talk to people'.

Look back at the work you are doing with your thought record. Do you notice any repeating patterns for the critical way(s) you describe yourself? What negative beliefs about yourself do your negative thoughts reflect?

Where you remain unsure as to what is really going on for you, here is another excellent technique to use.

The 'downward arrow' technique

Take any thought from your thought record, and apply a downward arrow to it in the following way.

In the example on the next page, you are worried about a party you have accepted to go to, and are beginning to feel very nervous. Using this skill, you have uncovered a core belief (two, in fact) that you have about yourself and which you can now work on. You can also ask yourself another question: 'What is the personal meaning to me if this does or doesn't occur?' Your answer might be: 'I am totally unlikable.'

Does this make sense to you, as a useful, probing technique? Practise it a great deal — it is actually a vital component in ensuring that you are working on the 'causal' thought or belief (this is simply the thought or belief that is truly responsible for how you are feeling) and not on some superficial idea that won't be relevant to helping you feel better.

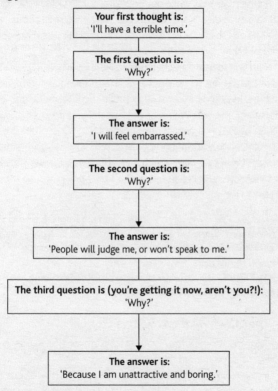

Your first thought is:
'I'll have a terrible time.'

The first question is:
'Why?'

The answer is:
'I will feel embarrassed.'

The second question is:
'Why?'

The answer is:
'People will judge me, or won't speak to me.'

The third question is (you're getting it now, aren't you?!):
'Why?'

The answer is:
'Because I am unattractive and boring.'

An example of the Downward Arrow Technique.

Once you have identified any basic, self-critical beliefs, you can begin to start chipping away at them, and replacing them with more helpful and realistic, positive beliefs. In this way, your self-esteem and self-acceptance will increase greatly.

Use the suggestions we have made above to continue to look at self-critical beliefs you may have about yourself. Especially look for beliefs that you have held for a long time.

If these beliefs stem from childhood, recall any particular words of criticism that you may have absorbed.

Strategies for replacing old beliefs with new ones

Start by focusing on your strengths and good points. Revisit Chapter 1 where we asked you to list ten personal qualities. We would now like you to add a further ten. You will need to refer back to them, so keep them by you.

Now write down your smallest achievements, abilities and personal qualities. We want you to get used to focusing on your *strengths* rather than your *weaknesses*. This is not something you will normally do, so it will not come naturally or easily – all the more reason for doing it! For example:

Look at your working days. Whether you are home-based or office-based, there will be plenty of examples on a daily basis of things you are quite good at (perhaps typing, cooking, keeping things neat, staying calm when others are getting worked up). Once you start thinking over the last week, you should not find it difficult.

Incorporate things you may like about yourself – 'I am kind', 'I am patient' – as well as things you can do. Don't rate your abilities and qualities. You don't have to be the best at anything before you write it down. Even being quite modest at something counts as a positive: 'I don't get too worked up when people are late' or 'I managed to stick to my diet for a week' all count.

One of the goals of this exercise is to get you to focus differently. Remember what you have learned – it is not who you are or what happened – it is your *perceptions* of who you are or what happened that define your thinking and your self-esteem.

You are now learning to shift your perceptions from negative to positive.

What you have *also* achieved is to collect a body of evidence to help you ditch your self-critical beliefs. Keep this evidence with you and move on to the next step.

Bringing positive qualities into focus with a positive data log

A positive data log (PDL) is an excellent tool for getting you to question self-critical beliefs. It is simple, but very effective. Take a negative belief that you hold, and – to start with – find any evidence you can that might suggest your belief is not true all the time. You can use some of the evidence that you collected previously. Use the chart on the next page. An example might be:

Self-critical belief: *I am unlikable.*
New, alternative belief: *I am quite likable.*
Evidence to support your new belief and weaken your old belief:
I do have a few friends.
I have been invited to several social occasions so far this year.
In general, people are pleasant to me.
My work colleagues are friendly and I get invited to workplace social functions.
I do my best to be kind and thoughtful.
My neighbour thanked me for my helpfulness.
I normally have a steady partner and I have been in two long-term relationships.
Although I said 'No', I have had a marriage proposal.
I am close to my family.

We have not suggested too big a swing from negative belief to positive belief. Changing beliefs can take several months, so a 'middle of the road' alternative will serve you better than to start with than an unrealistic, 'I am totally likable'. Now give this a go for yourself.

Start filling in your positive data log. We suggest you make up two or three, and gradually add to your evidence for each one over a period of a week or two, as you observe events and experiences that support them.

Positive data log

Self-critical belief: _____

New, alternative belief: _____

Evidence to support your new belief and weaken your old belief

1 _____
2 _____
3 _____
4 _____
5 _____
6 _____
7 _____
8 _____
9 _____
10 _____
11 _____
12 _____
13 _____
14 _____
15 _____
16 _____
17 _____
18 _____
19 _____
20 _____

Measure the improving strength of your new beliefs by rating them. Self-critical beliefs take longer to change than our day-to-day, event-specific negative thinking. This is, as you have already learned, because they have been around a lot longer and are more absolute.

However, you will begin to see some change fairly quickly and you will gain encouragement from using a rating scale to track this. Don't go for 100% – it's unrealistic and unattractive!

A 100% gain would be both difficult to achieve and undesirable. For example: if your original, self-critical belief was, 'I am unlikable' and the belief you would like to replace it with is, 'I am likable most of the time' (note we are not striving for a total opposite, but a realistic alternative) then your rating scale might look like this:

Desired belief: 'I am likable most of the time.'
Initial strength of that belief: (place a X over the percentage)

X
0%   25%   50%   75%   100%

Desired belief: 'I am likable most of the time.'
Strength of belief after two weeks of skills practice:

                        X
0%   25%   50%   75%   100%

Of course, these are subjective ratings, but you will have a very good 'feel' for how you are progressing, and by continuing to use your thought record and positive data log, you will find that you are gathering more and more evidence to support your new beliefs. You are training your mind to refocus on your more positive characteristics, and to re-evaluate the accuracy of your negative beliefs.

Exercise

Rate your self-critical beliefs as you see them now. You may find that, immediately, you don't really want to put your X over 0%. Place it on the scale as accurately as you can.

What does the fact that not all your crosses are on zero tell you about your thinking?

4

defeat low self-esteem by developing self-acceptance

The work you have done so far requires you to look squarely at your negative thoughts and behaviours and to dispute these – to challenge their truth, to look at alternative possibilities, and to check out evidence to support (in most instances) more balanced thinking. Self-acceptance is a different approach. Instead of arguing with your negative thoughts, you consider them as possibly realistic and truthful – you may even agree with some them.

You may think that this flies in the face of everything we've already said. But think again. This kind of self-acceptance enables you to conquer your Personal Fault Finder by saying: 'That's fine. I don't mind about these particular things I am no good at. I can accept my shortcomings *without* diminishing myself.'

If you can learn to do this with calm, inner peace – and even a little humour – the results can be quite spectacular.

The secret

The secret of true self-acceptance is to stop seeing ourselves as a single entity. We are all made up of hundreds of component parts – our skills, abilities, physique, sporting or artistic leanings, levels of competitiveness, intelligence, emotional maturity, personal qualities (such as kindness, compassion, generosity or meanness, good or poor humour) – and many more. To rate ourselves based on each of these individual strengths and weaknesses, we would have very varied ratings for them all. Some might be 8 or 9 out of 10, others perhaps just 1 or 2. If we add up our grand total of individual ratings, the figure we end up with is probably similar to that of most other people – even though our areas of strengths and weaknesses might be totally unalike.

Exercise

* Draw a line down the centre of a piece of paper.
* In the first column write down as many personal skills and characteristics as you can think of.
* In the second column, give yourself a subjective rating out of 10 (where 0 = useless, 10 = my best feature). Don't be falsely modest (you don't have to show this to anyone).
* Just for fun, add your scores up and see what the grand total is.
* What do you think you might discover if you do this?
* This exercise becomes more interesting if you suggest to another friend or family member that they try it as well – using the same basic criteria.

Healthy versus unhealthy self-acceptance

Healthy self-acceptance encourages you to accept *specific* weaknesses about yourself – while at the same time rejecting the idea that having these weaknesses makes you an overall no-hoper. People suffering from depression tend to have an unhealthy lack of self-acceptance, and see themselves as generally worthless. A more optimistic personality will reflect only on specific areas of weakness, and not see these weaknesses as meaning that they are not 'up to scratch' in general terms.

Someone with an unhealthy lack of self-acceptance will consider their weaknesses untenable, and revert to the idea of global uselessness. Healthy self-acceptance embraces acknowledging your weaknesses while not writing yourself off because of them. You understand that it is okay to have skills deficits, make mistakes, get things wrong or not have the strengths of the next person. You say, 'This is called being human, as we all are' and you retain your self-respect.

An unhealthy lack of self-acceptance does not encourage change. It allows its followers to stay as they are, lost in self-criticism and low self-esteem. Their ideas conform to the view that there is no point in trying when failure is a certainty. Or they are 'all talk' – the diet/exercise regime/study course starts tomorrow, and tomorrow never comes. Healthy self-acceptance gives you energy and motivation to change. Accepting weaknesses does not mean *retaining* weaknesses. Change is seen as positive, and accepting your shortcomings without any loss of self-esteem will enable you to meet the challenges it provides you with.

Exercise

Jot down three or four of your perceived personal weaknesses. Now, for each one, ask yourself two questions:
  * 'Does having this weakness make me a useless/bad/ insignificant person?'
  * 'Am I doing anything towards improving this weakness?'
Answering 'Yes' to the first question and 'No' to the second means you have unhealthy self-acceptance. Answering 'No' to the first and 'Yes' to the second means the opposite (and well done!)

Big I, little i

Exercise to help you understand self-acceptance: big I, little i

Here is a question for you: Is a zebra a black animal with white stripes, or a white animal with black stripes?

Write your answer down. We'll come back to this in the next step.

* Now look at the big 'I' below. For the purposes of this exercise, this is you! It represents everything about you that makes your totality as a human being. Draw a larger scale version of this big 'I' on a piece of paper.

* Now think about qualities that you have – ones that you are aware of yourself, or that your family and friends might consider to be your good points (such as intelligent or a snappy dresser). Write a little 'i' inside the big 'I' for each of these.

* Move on to your weaknesses – again, both those that you perceive yourself to have, and those which family and friends might consider you to have (such as no humour or often arrives late). Write further little 'i's inside the big 'I' for each of these.

* What about neutral aspects of yourself? For example, you can cut the grass, dress reasonably, are of average height, have brown hair, do not turn up late too often, and so on. Write more little 'i's in for these.

Once you have done all this, your big 'I' should look like this.

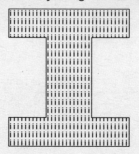

Of all the weaknesses that came to mind, which one currently bothers you the most? Which one makes you dislike yourself the most, feel ashamed of yourself and wish you were different? Now circle one of the little 'i's to represent this.

Now look again at your big 'I' – yourself. The little 'i's within it are the sum total of yourself as a human being: good, bad, neutral – literally warts and all. The circled aspect is just one of many – hundreds, if you took the time to keep working on this.

So does this mean you are a good person or a bad person? A success or a failure? Think about it, and we will look at this further in the next step, when we return to the question of the zebra.

What did you learn from the big 'I', little 'i' exercise? We hope you will have gathered that you are far too complex an individual to be able to rate yourself in any one way. This is the principle of self-acceptance – you learn not to rate or evaluate yourself, but to appreciate that you are made up of hundreds of different facets that are constantly changing, and defy any sort of generalized, global assessment of yourself based on these.

However, this does not mean that you cannot rate individual aspects of yourself. Indeed, self-acceptance encourages this, as doing so allows you to consider whether you would like to make changes and improvements to these aspects – but without running yourself down for having these weaknesses in the first place. For example, perhaps you would like to improve your time keeping?

Fallibility

We are *all* fallible. It's what makes us human. We probably make far more mistakes in life than we accept or acknowledge – or even notice. Many of us keep repeating these same mistakes again and again. This doesn't make us bad people or total idiots; it makes us fallible human beings – in other words, *normal*.

The zebra

How did you get on with the question of the zebra? Did it seem impossible to make a definite answer? Thinking about our discussion at present, how might that fit in? Could it mean that it is as difficult to say something is either black or white as it is to say that we are personally useless or perfect, nasty or nice, hopeless or wonderful? The answer to this is, almost certainly, 'Yes'.

Before we leave the zebra, you will recall that in previous steps we have referred a great deal to challenging assumptions, and finding different ways of thinking about things. The question of the zebra illustrates this beautifully. As you ponder over the question, what about this for an answer?

The zebra is neither a black animal with white stripes, nor a white animal with black stripes, but a pink animal with black and white stripes.

Never stop looking for an alternative way of thinking about things!

Exercise

* Write down two or three weaknesses that you would like to fix, in the light of what we have learned.
* Rate how badly you feel about having these weaknesses from 1 to 10 (where 1 = very bad, 10 = fine).

Do you think you have been kinder to yourself with these ratings than you might have been before you read this chapter on self-acceptance?

We hope that, by now, you can consider the idea that you do not have a particular global rating as a human being. Rather, you are (as we all are) simply made up of a huge number of different qualities and characteristics – some of which are strengths, some of which are neutral and some of which are weaknesses. We hope this has helped you see yourself in a more accepting light.

Here are a few more basic illustrations to ensure you are thinking on the right lines.

Picture a bowl of fruit with all your favourites in it – apples, oranges, pears, grapes, peaches – whichever you like the best. Look at the bowl closely. Wait a moment – there's a bad fruit in there: a grape with mould or an apple with a worm-hole. What will you do? Throw the whole bowl of fruit away, or simply throw away the mouldy grape or wormy apple, and keep the rest? If the latter, then why write yourself off as a person, rather than accepting or working on an individual weakness?

Imagine that, when you go into work tomorrow, the receptionist tells you that you are a green frog. What a load of nonsense! Then you go to a meeting, and everyone in the meeting tells you that you are a green frog. How absurd! This is obviously a practical joke that your colleagues are all in on.

How interesting it is that when people tell you that you are a green frog, you are resolute in not believing it. This is because you are retaining your powers of discrimination. Yet when you make a mistake, you label yourself as totally stupid or useless – *losing* your powers of discrimination (which would otherwise be telling you that messing up once does not mean you are a total idiot).

Think about what you have read in this chapter, and begin to practise this new, very enlightening outlook. It will help you develop your self-acceptance enormously, as it will give you permission to be fallible and human without seeing yourself as a failure. It also establishes that you are not alone and that we are all quite fallible and may make many mistakes in life. This is normality – not the perfectionism that we can wrongly assume should define us.

5

defeat low self-esteem through rejecting victimhood

It can be all too easy for us to blame other people or, more vaguely, 'circumstances' for our unhappiness and feelings of self-esteem. It's all too easy, too, for us to rely on others – very often a partner, relation or close friend – to make us feel good about ourselves. Comforting as such an approach can be, it can ultimately be self-defeating. Habitually playing the victim and depending too much on others for our sense of self-worth can make us powerless and vulnerable.

Accepting responsibility, not necessarily for what happens to you (no one can quite control that!), but for how you respond to what happens to you – for your thoughts, emotions and behaviours – is an important key to healthy self-esteem. This is emotional intelligence – it's you who is in control, who has the self-awareness to manage your emotions. . . This can be an enormously liberating and positive step to take. Do it!

The low self-esteem victim

How you perceive what goes on around you, and how you interpret your abilities to deal with issues, has a great impact on self-esteem.

Jenny's story

Jenny was in a troubled relationship, and her partner, James, had recently moved out of their shared home. Although James had treated her quite cruelly at times, having several affairs and behaving in a moody and erratic way, Jenny's self-esteem was so low that she interpreted this as simply a response to her own hopelessness and 'unlovability'.

Jenny spent a great deal of time telephoning and emailing James, begging him to come home. She felt that, without him, she was totally unlovable, and that she needed him desperately to restore her confidence.

In the end, James reluctantly agreed to Jenny's pleading, and returned home. However, the relationship continued to deteriorate, as James did not really want to be there, and continued to see other women.

Jenny's despair came from feeling absolutely stuck. She felt she had tried as hard as she could in the relationship, and that it was James' cruel treatment that made her feel so poorly about herself.

If only James would change, she would feel okay about herself again. Without his input, Jenny felt unable to deal with her life.

This is victim mode: 'I feel so badly due to someone else's behaviour, and need them to change in order to feel better.'

Of course, we may receive an increase in our personal 'feel-good factor' when people treat us well, but we cannot rely on this. The moment we say, 'If he had not done that, I would not have felt this way', 'I only acted that way because of the way she behaved' or 'If she would only treat me with more respect, I'd feel so much better', we are trapped in a way of thinking that prevents us from taking responsibility and making changes.

You will continue to suffer from low self-esteem if you blame anyone else for making you feel the way that you do. You may be right; so-and-so may be rude, may have run you down terribly, may have landed you in it, made you look a fool, or whatever. But it is not about what other people do, it is about how you respond to what they do that decides whether you feel a helpless victim or not.

Exercise

Think about the last time someone had let you down, for example cancelling an engagement at the last minute.
   * Did you feel a victim? In other words, did you feel that the actions of the other person were to blame for how you felt?
   * Was this a 'one off' or do you often feel this way?
   * What might you do differently the next time it happens?

We briefly referred to over-personalization in Chapter 3. Examples of over-personalization are:
   * A friend makes a comment about liking long hair, and you immediately think they are criticizing your new short cut.
   * Your manager tells you that the department is lagging behind completing an important project on time and you assume he is commenting on your own poor performance.
When you over-personalize, you erroneously feel that you are personally to blame for the perceived negative reactions of others: 'If someone disagrees with me, then I must be wrong, and that makes me stupid.'

This is not good for self-esteem. You must identify these thoughts and counteract them. This involves using some of the broader thinking skills we discussed in earlier chapters, such as:
   * Have respect for the opinions of others, as you hope they will respect yours.

* Distinguish between opinion and fact. However strongly either you, or the person talking to you, believe something, that doesn't make it true.
* Have confidence in your own views.
* Others have their own problems.

Remember, other people don't always react in the best possible way. This has nothing to do with you.

Exercise

Think back over the recent past to an occasion when you might have erroneously taken something too personally.
* What went through your mind?
* How strongly did you believe it? Give yourself a score on a scale from 1 to 10 (where 1 = mildly and 10 = very strongly).
* Consider some alternative ways of thinking about this, using some of the skills we have mentioned above.
* How do you feel now? Give yourself a score on a scale from 1 to 10 (where 1 = devastated and 10 = fine).

Self-pity: blaming yourself rather than others

Every time you run yourself down, you are indulging in self-pity. Not very attractive, is it?

Self-pity is similar to getting locked into victim mode, except on this occasion, you are not blaming others as much as you are blaming yourself – and feeling sorry for yourself.

When you think this way, you are allowing your PFF free rein, and not even arguing with it; it is easier to say 'Poor me' and leave it at that.

Don't! Most of us have 'wallowing' periods. Of course, you are allowed these occasionally. But use them sparingly, and be aware that you are choosing to do so. This will give you breathing space to pull yourself together and look at what you are doing.

* When did you last feel sorry for yourself? Why?
* Do you still feel that way – if not, why not?
* What did you do to stop your self-pitying thoughts?
* How did you feel once they had disappeared?

Taking responsibility for your feelings

One of the easiest ways of getting rid of feelings of victimization or self-pity is to take responsibility for ourselves.

It is not difficult. Look in the mirror and say this: 'I now take full responsibility for my happiness.'

Now say this: 'No one except me is responsible for my happiness.'

There you go! Okay, we do appreciate that it is not quite this easy, but it *almost* is.

Jim's story

Jim was walking down the corridor at work, when a colleague coming the other way jostled him, resulting in hot coffee being spilled over Jim's new suit. Instead of apologizing, the colleague made a weak joke about it and rushed on, calling back to Jim that he was late for a meeting but that Jim should send him the bill for the dry cleaning. Jim was furious. He was left to clean up the mess, dry himself off, and had to walk into a meeting himself looking a wreck. In response to a jokey comment made by someone in the meeting concerning Jim's appearance, he hit the roof and was asked by the Chairperson to leave the room and calm down. Jim's anger had taken over. He blamed his colleagues for his wretched day and the anger it had produced that seemed to alienate him from several of them.

Was he right? As we are sure you realize, the only person responsible for Jim's anger was Jim himself.

Once we realize that no one else has control over how we feel – and that we have excellent control over how we feel – we can put the lid on negative emotions. You don't have to. If you wish to be angry or upset, be angry or upset. But you are choosing to do so, so make these choices through valid thinking, not using 'I couldn't help it' as an excuse.

With the exception of reflex actions such as a knee jerk or blushing, we can control our responses. It may be hard, but it can be done. This is called 'emotional intelligence', which means that we are able to identify and manage our emotions so that we use them appropriately, rather than let inappropriate emotions take charge of our thinking and actions; this can in turn lead to upset, both for ourselves and others and thus lower our sense of self-worth.

Learn to take emotional responsibility. You will feel much better for it.

Exercise

Do you always take responsibility for your emotions? Look back over the last two weeks (longer, if need be).

Was there a time when you felt extremely emotional about something? If so, can you recall what thoughts were in your mind?

Did they perhaps include the idea that someone or something had made you feel that way?

How could you look at that now, taking responsibility for it yourself?

Don't give up

This chapter of the book has looked at our weakness to apportion blame as an explanation for our poor self-esteem, rather than taking responsibility and making changes. One of the main reasons that people don't change – or not as much as they want to – is that they give up. It is natural to hope that when you open a self-help book, a load of fairy dust will fall out over you to make everything okay, or that reading it once will 'do the trick'. But like everything else, it is regular practice that is important.

Giving up can take you back into the victim or self-pitying mode:
* 'It's too hard.'
* 'I don't have time.'
* 'It doesn't make sense.'
* 'It doesn't work.'

Research shows it takes approximately 21 days to break an old, destructive habit or form a new, positive habit. Please keep this in mind.

It will no doubt take you at least that long to gain positive benefits from what you do. While you will understand the book immediately, acting on it is harder. You may read a section and say 'I know that'. But actually, you don't *really* know it.

In order to *really* know it, it must become part of your thinking, your emotions, your actions and reactions. So unless this is the case, reading something and understanding it is not enough.

Exercise

In the last year, what have you given up, and why? Write these items down and think about each one in turn for a moment. There will no doubt be good and valid reasons for some, but not for all.
* When have you used any of the negative thought ideas we have suggested above?
* Do you have any regrets about some of the things you gave up?
* How has this affected your self-esteem?
* What do you learn from this?

To obtain the best benefit, continue reading through this book in its entirety. Then go back to the sections that particularly deal with specific problems you know you have trouble with. Think about these steps deeply, and most importantly, *act* on them.

This is about taking responsibility for your development. This is how you will increase your self-esteem. Don't make excuses; this is what victims do – don't fall back into 'I couldn't help it' syndrome. You can. And you will succeed.

6

increase your self-esteem through assertiveness

The ability to be assertive is a sure sign of healthy self-esteem – your opinion counts and you know it, and you are prepared to negotiate calmly in order to achieve your goals. Passivity, by contrast, is likely to be a sign of poor self-esteem – you avoid conflict because you are unsure how to handle yourself and really don't believe your opinion is worth much anyway.

However, being assertive is certainly not to be confused with being aggressive or bullying (too many people make this basic mistake). In fact, it's quite the opposite – it's about *taking control* of your emotions and your behaviour in a planned, measured way, seeing the other person's point of view and, in the end, probably reaching some kind of compromise.

In this chapter, you'll learn about the four main behavioural attitudes and how you can train yourself not only to act assertively but to think assertively too.

The role of assertiveness in good self-esteem

Does dealing with interpersonal (for example social or work-based) situations that might have a degree of conflict in them cause you to feel inadequate? Do you avoid these situations at all costs, feel you are always on the losing end, or show yourself up in a poor light? Do you currently:

* find yourself getting upset very quickly when others question your opinions and views?
* avoid discussions that might become confrontational, even though it might mean you don't achieve something you need or want?
* make a comment then immediately wish you had not?
* agree with the wishes of others – when really you don't agree at all?
* feel your self-esteem constantly dented by your inability to stand up to other people's arguments?

With good self-esteem these thoughts will disappear. Learning assertiveness skills will give you much increased self-confidence. They will also help you to:

* improve your image and credibility
* behave more tactfully
* feel less stressed about confrontation
* achieve desired outcomes in a positive way.

Assertiveness skills

If you do not already possess these assertiveness skills – and most people with poor self-esteem do not – then you will need to practise them a great deal. This in itself may trigger anxiety in some of you, so here is a strategy for making it much easier.

Get a voice recorder with a good microphone, and you can practise ahead of time, saying what you want to say without anyone telling you not to be so foolish.

We often mentally rehearse what we want to say to someone, so how much better to do it so that you can hear how it sounds, and revise it if you need to? Self-criticism in this instance is not another day out for your PFF, it is a positive move on your part. Listen to how you sound:

* Are you saying too much... or too little?
* Are you sounding too weak... or too strident?

Whatever you don't like, note it, and then have another go again. Eventually, it will become easy and automatic.

Exercise: assertiveness questionnaire

Take the test below, which will help you check whether you deal with things assertively or not. Give yourself a score from 1 to 3 for each statement (where 1 = never, or not like me, 2 = sometimes like me, 3 = always, or very like me).

A

When I have to confront someone about a problem I feel very nervous. ☐

I am easily upset or intimidated by ridicule or sarcasm. ☐

Being liked by people is very important to me no matter what the cost. ☐

I really don't like conflict and will avoid it any way I can. ☐

I find it hard to be direct with people if I think they will not like what I have to say. ☐

Total score for this section ☐

B

I lose my temper easily. ☐

I don't care if people like me as long as I get what I want. ☐

I'll use the tone of my voice or sarcasm to get what I want from other people. ☐

Patience with people is not one of my strong points. ☐

I often wag my finger at other people to make my point. ☐

Total score for this section ☐

C

I remain calm when faced with sarcasm, ridicule or criticism from others. ☐

I am not frightened of addressing problems directly without casting blame. ☐

I am confident about asking for what I want, or explaining how I feel. ☐

I am able to look other people in the eye when dealing with difficult issues. ☐

I feel confident in my ability to handle confrontational work situations. ☐

Total score for this section ☐

D

I often make my point by using sarcasm. ☐

Rather than speaking out directly to make my feelings known, I'll use impatient or 'cutting' remarks. ☐

I show my impatience by my body language. ☐

If asked to do something I don't want to, I'll do it, but deliberately won't make any great effort. ☐

I use silence to make people realize I am upset. ☐

Total score for this section ☐

Take the test and tot up your scores for each section. Next, you will learn what this means about you.

You may have an idea already what your scores tell you. Now let's put them into a specific context so that you have a clearer idea of where you 'fit'.

Using your scores from the test, identify which of the behaviour types most apply to you – the higher you score in a particular section (A, B, C or D), the more applicable that behaviour type is to you. You might find that you are a combination of two or three, rather than always acting in the same way.

The four behaviour types

The test you took was based on identifying which of four different behaviour types you adhered to most closely. The types are:

A Passive
B Aggressive
C Assertive
D Passive aggressive

Passive behaviour

When we behave passively, we tend to 'let things go'. We may totally disagree with what is going on, but don't say anything. If we do speak, we are usually disproportionately deferential, full of premature apology, and back down too easily.

Aggressive behaviour

Bully boy tactics, rudeness, raised voice, shouting, threats – all to ensure that the aggressor gets their way. You may have behaved this way yourself on occasion, even if you usually exhibit passivity. For the passive person, not saying what they mean can eventually lead to emotional overload. Something 'snaps' and suddenly Sally Shy hits the roof and becomes Betty Bully.

Passive-aggressive behaviour

One of the most common examples of this is 'the silent treatment'. Here, we are not being overtly aggressive but using silence, sulking, leaving a room when the other person walks in, being deliberately obstructive. The objective of P-A is to get one's own way by making the other party or parties feel guilty.

Assertive behaviour

When you behave assertively, you remain (relatively) calm and stand your ground.

You are also willing to hear the points of view of others, as you don't feel threatened or intimidated by them. Valid counter arguments might make you change your point of view, but if not you clearly stay with what you believe in. You treat others with respect. You may be willing to compromise, you speak clearly and you are willing to persist with the discussion until a satisfactory outcome is reached.

Exercise

Write down at least one example, over the last week or two, where you consider you have behaved in each of the above behaviour styles. Most of us vary, rarely using one style the whole time.

Recall how you felt after each event, and rate which felt the best, with regard to how you felt about yourself afterwards. What do you learn from this?

Thinking assertively

When we behave assertively, we focus on outcomes and results rather than emotions. Look back to the last chapter when we discussed managing our emotions using emotional intelligence. This is exactly what you are required to do here.

Before you can behave assertively, you need to *think* assertively, you need to be able to consider the outcomes and results you want, ahead of time. These outcomes and results don't simply include getting what you want. They should also include:

* how you feel about yourself and the other person
* how he or she feels about you
* whether the outcome you have worked for has improved your relationship for the future or enhanced mutual respect. In other words, whether it has left your self-esteem in good shape.

Thinking assertively is important since it starts off the train of situation-emotions-behaviour-outcome, and is a point at which you can maintain control and get the situation to work in your favour, rather than against you.

Think of a situation where you will need to use good negotiating skills to achieve the outcome you want. Now write down what that outcome is and, using the example method above, write a sentence or two under each heading to show how it might go, and what thinking skills you would use to ensure a good outcome.

Behaving assertively

Once you have mastered these skills, you will be able to:
* confront difficult issues with others
* stay in control of your emotions while you do this
* stand your ground when the going gets tough.

Use the following three-step process as a format for negotiation where you need to act assertively.

1. Acknowledge the other person's point of view

Most people will expect you to 'come at them' with your own arguments and views, so they will be surprised when you first of all reflect an understanding of their problem. For example, it might be an unrealistic work deadline that your boss has imposed on you. An acknowledgement might be: 'The work we are doing now is for our biggest client, and I appreciate your concern that we get this project in on time for them.'

Acknowledging sets the scene for dialogue, rather than confrontation. You are actually indicating that you are on the same side as your boss, and share his goals.

2. State your own position

If you really cannot meet the deadline, then you must stand your ground on this point. It is often useful to start this step with the words 'however' or 'but', so that you now have: '. . .I appreciate your concern that we get this project in on time for them. *However* even working solely on this project and nothing else, the time scale is unachievable, if we are to produce good work.'

3. Offer a solution

Sometimes an obvious alternative is not readily available. However, remember that this is about results, and actually there has to be a solution – even if it is that the work does not get done on time. So your thinking needs to move from 'I can't possibly achieve this' to 'What can we do?' and state the possibilities.

Using these steps achieves these vital things:

* It enables mutual understanding of the problems.
* It gives you the respect of the other person.
* It prevents you from being forced to accept an unrealistic/unacceptable/unwanted situation.
* It encourages a solution that will suit both parties.
* Your emotions don't get the better of you and cause you to feel upset/angry/disappointed, thus denting your self-esteem.
* The feel-good factor at the outcome is huge, and excellent for confidence-building.

Exercise

Now find a situation and practise the three-step process.

You don't need to wait for a major confrontation, even negotiating over a cup of coffee is a good start and will get you used to it. You may also wish to practise this with your voice recorder.

Think of possible responses you might get, and work on how to deal with them assertively.

Your assertive rights

Thinking assertively means reminding yourself of your basic rights, and then being comfortable with them. Lists of 'rights' can be very long, so here we just wish to remind you of your right to be a normal, fallible human being, and to ensure you appreciate that this makes you just like everybody else and perfectly okay!

Just also remember three things:

1 Rights carry responsibilities. If you choose the right to go to bed late, don't grumble when it is hard to get up in the morning.
2 Others have rights as well. Don't let this deter you from saying your piece, but be prepared for the other person to say theirs as well (and that's fine, by the way).
3 See issues from the other person's point of view as well as your own.

Exercise

You can practise getting comfortable with your rights by doing the following exercise:

Think of a 'right'	How you view that right with low self-esteem	How to view it with a more assertive viewpoint
I have the right to say how I feel	What I have to say is probably less important than what others have to say. I will be interrupted, spoken over, ignored.	My views are just as valuable as anyone else's. I will use my assertive skills to overcome interruptions and persist with my point of view, while acknowledging what others have to say.

Copy the chart above and fill in three more examples of rights you consider important to your self-esteem. Use the thought challenging columns to counter your concerns with some assertive views.

Assertiveness is a key skill for defeating low self-esteem. As with everything, it really is little more than a matter of practice. So do go ahead: practise as much as you can, and your confidence will soar.

7

act your way to good self-esteem

A good way to improve your self-esteem is to *pretend* to have it. Your PFF will encourage you to look around at others and point out how confident they are – and how lacking in self-esteem you are in comparison. You are not going to teach yourself now how to check the validity of those thoughts – you have hopefully already done a lot of work on that – but rather to learn how to *appear* just as confident as everyone else – many of whom will be 'faking it' successfully, just as you will be.

A plus of pretending is that, after a while, we don't have to pretend anymore. It becomes natural. Telling yourself you are confident when you are not is an untruth. But the more you tell it – and, in this case, *practise* it – the more you will believe it. You will gradually find it easier and easier, and feel less and less self-conscious. So let's start pretending . . .

Master confident body language

When we communicate, over 50% of the message we give comes from our body language, or non-verbal communication. You can therefore send out confident, positive messages without having to say a word.

How would you recognize confidence from body language? How would you recognize lack of confidence from body language? Consider a few ideas of your own, and then look at the list below.

Non-confident body language	Confident body language
Crossing your arms	Open and expansive
Hugging your body	Good posture
Crossing your legs	Leaning towards someone
Placing a hand under your chin	Standing asymmetrically
Stooped posture	Relaxed stance
Standing far from the other person	Leaning towards the other person

* Imagine a string running through your body, right up out of the top of your head. Imagine someone pulling this string tight. This will cause you to stand straighter and taller, which always gives a confident impression.
* Clasp your hands casually in front of you – don't fold them across your body. You will look more relaxed this way.
* Give a confident first impression by shaking hands firmly with the other person.
* Moderate use of hand gestures can help to convey meaning when you are speaking.

Practise confident body language in front of the mirror at home. Get an idea of how you look using different stances.

You can also use the list of 'no-no's' to see how unconfident you look in these positions.

If you wish to enlist the help of family or friends, you could ask someone to video you acting out a situation with someone else. This would be particularly useful if you have a special function to attend that is unnerving you.

Cultivate a confident expression

Conveying confidence and warmth through your facial expression will make connecting with others much easier.

Eye contact

Eye contact is an important ingredient of a confident expression, but can be hard to get right, especially if you feel nervous – while pretending not to be. It is important because it shows that you wish to communicate with the other person and are interested in what they have to say. So look people in the eye not only when you are speaking, but also when they are – this will also help you to gauge their reactions and respond accordingly. Too much eye contact can seem rather aggressive and overpowering: too little can make you seem nervous or embarrassed. A good rule of thumb is to maintain eye contact for about 60%–70% of the time.

Smile

Smile! Not only does smiling (appropriately, of course) make you appear warm and friendly, research has shown that smiling will help you to feel more self-confident. Picture someone coming towards you with a warm smile on their face. Nothing could convey 'I'm delighted to see you' more strongly. It is easy to do, and makes a huge difference.

Relax

Adopt a relaxed and friendly expression. This of course can be easier said than done, and has to be linked, up to a point, to your basic personality.

Exercise

Practise facial expressions in the mirror.

Say a few words and sentences out loud and be aware of how you look when you say these things.

Have a go at making statements with a smile (where the content would be appropriate) and see what difference that makes to how you look and how you feel as you speak the words. You will find it makes you feel much more confident.

Develop a confident-sounding voice

This is not about what you say, but the way that you say it. Nervousness is very audible through the tone of your voice – you may stutter, the pitch may go up or you may speak in a garbled way. Practise controlling your voice and relaxing to reduce anxiety and nerves.

Slow down!

It is better to say nothing than to say too much that sounds bad. Return to Chapter 6 on assertiveness to review your confidence in being able to present well without having to say too much.

Not too loud!

Something else that happens to our voice when we are nervous is that it gets too loud, or too soft. Simply becoming aware of this when you are speaking will help you adjust your volume button. You can also ask close family.

Not too fast!

Another weakness of nervousness is that we tend to speak too fast. This is less common than speaking too loudly or too softly, but you need to check whether you do this. You can use self-awareness, or ask someone else.

Keep the pitch low

A low, clear voice indicates confidence, while a high voice will indicate nervousness. Practise varying the pitch of your voice while speaking into a voice recorder. Listen to authoritative speakers such as newsreaders, and notice when they especially lower their voices.

Exercise

Developing an awareness of how you speak requires lots of practice. Do so in the following ways:

* Think about your tone of voice when you are in a conversation.
* Spend some time with your voice recorder – most people are extremely surprised by how they sound. It is not usually what they expected.
* Enlist family and friends if you can – both to comment on your speech in different circumstances, and to role play conversations with you in situations you find most difficult to come across well in.

First impressions

Whatever happens later, first impressions are the most highly significant factor on which others will assess you – and you them. Think what happens when you meet someone new. You immediately look for signs and signals that will categorize them in your mind. To project confidence yourself, work on the following.

Dressing appropriately

Don't take the view that how you dress doesn't matter. It may matter to other people, and only an extremely naturally confident person (which we assume you are not) would take the view that they really don't care what others think. You do want to make a good first impression, because it will make you feel more confident. So dress appropriately to the situation. If you really don't know what that is, don't guess – ask.

Signalling confidence

Ensure that your body language shows the same confidence as your facial expression. During the 'first impressions' stage, you will be judged much more on body language than on what you say, for example: saying 'How nice to be here', while your body language is defensive and your face taut with nerves is not going to wash. People will judge your behaviour more than your words at this point.

Other points to focus on to get the first impression right are:

* a firm handshake; where appropriate (it isn't always, of course) this indicates excellent self-confidence
* a broad smile; nothing says 'Pleased to meet you' better than this
* good eye contact.

Exercise

Think about social/work situations that make you especially nervous. Now consider the last time you were in one of these situations:

Did you make any conscious, proactive attempt at making a good first impression, or did you simply worry about what impression you might be making?

Now replay this situation. What could you have done – or could you do in the future – to ensure that you make a good first impression, whatever you are feeling inside?

Faking confidence may sound both difficult and insincere. Neither is the case. As with assertiveness, it is all about practice.

Have a go at 'acting confident' in easy, non-threatening situations at first – even just in the local shop, or with the post person or your next door neighbour. Say a little more than you usually would; focus on your voice and especially on your body language. You will soon find that you are no longer acting, and that this is an easy way of being. Thus, what was initially artificial becomes genuine.

This will give you the confidence to 'act the part' in more difficult situations – perhaps at a party or at work – and literally test out what happens. How do others react to you? How do you feel afterwards? Very soon you will have a new 'default' and your self-esteem will rise with this.

body image

Poor body image is often found in those suffering from poor self-esteem and can be both cause and symptom. It can *cause* low self-esteem because people consider that what they believe to be their lack of physical attractiveness is getting in the way of finding a good relationship or of getting ahead in their career. It can be a *symptom* because all too often people with more general problems with self-esteem neglect their appearance because they don't consider themselves worth the effort. Sadly, such beliefs can be self-fulfilling and poor body image and low self-esteem can become locked in a vicious circle.

In this chapter we aim to show you how poor body image is just like any other distorted negative belief and is based on false assumptions and negative ways of thinking. In short, our body image has very little to do with our actual body and everything to do with attitude, and as such can be changed for the better.

Is your body image a problem?

Having difficulty liking your looks makes it harder to accept yourself, but you do not need to live this way. You can change your relationship with your body from one of active dislike to one of being relaxed and confident with your looks.

Exercise

To check whether body image is a problem for you, answer the following questions. For each question, rate your belief in the statement on a scale of 0–10 (where 0 = not at all and 10 = a lot).

1 Are you uncomfortable with your body in general?
2 Are there aspects of your physical appearance that you really dislike?
3 Do you spend a great deal of time worrying about what you look like?
4 Do you think that what you look like plays a great part in whether others like you or not?
5 Do you think that what you look like plays a part in how much you like yourself?
6 When you think of your looks, do the same negative thoughts keep cropping up?
7 Do these negative thoughts prevent you from enjoying day-to-day life?
8 Do you avoid certain activities or situations (visiting the gym, for example, or going swimming with others) because you feel self-conscious about how you look?
9 Are you considering (or have you had) cosmetic surgery for any part of your body?
10 Do you depend on clothes and/or cosmetics to try and disguise what you consider weaknesses in your appearance?
11 Are you endlessly searching for a new diet, the latest body-shaping exercise, a more flattering hairstyle or dress style?

12 Do you spend a lot of time, effort and money attempting to bolster up your imperfect looks?

Now tot up your score and see how you view your body.

0–30
Your body image is good. You don't need to read this chapter.

30–60
Your body image is moderately good, and you are not overly obsessive about it.

60–90
You have a poor body image and spend far too much time and effort in worrying about it and trying to change your physical appearance.

90–120
Your poor body image is spoiling your life. You may wish to consider professional help, if making changes alone seems too hard.

How did you score? Unless you discovered that your body image is excellent, now write down aspects of your physical appearance that really bother you. Do you feel that if you looked better, it would change how you feel about yourself in general? Jot down any ideas you have as to how you might deal with this problem.

How does poor body image affect you?

Many people with low self-esteem also suffer from poor body image. In what ways do you personally feel that your view of your physical appearance affects your life? Before reading further, note the ways in which your perceived physical imperfections affect you.

You may have come up with some of the following:
* My self-esteem is lowered generally.
* It causes much social anxiety, as I feel that others are negatively judging my looks all the time.

* It spoils my sex life, as I hate my partner seeing my body and feel inhibited when love-making.
* I feel depressed about my looks most of the time.
* It has caused me to suffer from eating disorders.

If you have discovered that you have an extremely poor body image, don't worry. This information will help you to make changes.

Say 'Goodbye' to poor body image

Poor body image is based on negative beliefs and assumptions (remember them from the early part of this book?) rather than reality. For example:

* a negative belief (a fairly absolute view) in relation to body image could be 'Good-looking people are more successful in life.'
* a negative assumption (more of an 'If. . . then' statement) might be 'If I were better looking, then my life would be much happier.'

You can challenge these ideas by finding alternative ways of viewing them; or if your more balanced viewpoint still isn't enough to sway your negative beliefs, you can focus on evidence that simply doesn't support your negative views.

Now we would like you to create a chart like the one below. Use this to record your negative beliefs, find evidence that challenge their truths and then, most importantly, replace them with more helpful beliefs about your own looks and the place of looks in society in general.

Challenging beliefs about your body image

My negative belief about my body image or the importance of good looks in society:
Evidence that disputes this belief:

Alternative belief that gives me a more positive view of my body image or the place of physical appearance in society:
How do I feel about my body image when I consider it this way?

Please note that we are not looking for you to provide a complete *volte face* here. That would be unrealistic and unbelievable. What we hope you will find is that you are, at the very least, starting to loosen your negative beliefs about yourself, and replacing them with more balanced ideas, and which make you feel somewhat better. It is actually important for you to work in this way, as being able to believe a different perception is vital to increasing your self-esteem.

To help you, here are some generic examples of the types of beliefs people with poor body image hold. Some may apply to you and there may be others that you hold that are not listed here. Use the chart to cover all of them:

* 'People judge my character by my looks.'
* 'My life would be much happier if I was better looking.'
* 'I am physically unattractive and I know other people see me that way as well.'
* 'My ... (part of body) is ... (too big, too small, etc.) and this is to blame for my low self-esteem.'
* 'There is nothing physically attractive about me at all.'

You will probably have many negative views specific to yourself. Work through them all.

Exercise

Once a day for a week, write down three physical features that you like about yourself. Focus on your smallest features, for example:

* Look at the shape of your ears ot the size of your wrists
* Do you have slim ankles?

* Are your toes well formed?
* What about your knees?
* How do you feel about the shape of your nose?
* You can even make perceived negatives into positives. If you are female and worry about a small bust, think how nice it will be when you are old not to suffer from saggy breasts!

This is the detail that we are looking for and you must complete three positive features every day for a week.

Once you have done this, repeat this exercise on a weekly basis: one evening a week, write down three attractive features about your physical appearance. You can repeat features, it does not matter. It is the principle of your thinking that will be changing. Don't make the mistake of thinking that this is too simplistic to be meaningful. It can be a very powerful exercise, with long-lasting results. Be pleased that something so simple can have such a strong effect!

Making changes

We do not wish to ignore the fact that one of the reasons why you may have a poor body image is that the reality you see in the mirror is confirming this for you.

If you strongly dislike how you look, it may be that, as well as an attitude adjustment, you do need to consider an appearance adjustment.

So why don't you? We all know an obese person whose 'diet starts tomorrow' and who never visits a gym. The problem here may be that low self-esteem is affecting their effort rating as well. Or it may be that there are hidden benefits in not shaping up, such as the excuses it provides for general inadequacy or lack of a relationship.

Be honest with yourself. Ask yourself firmly whether any of these situations apply to you. Are you simply failing to acknowledge that there are areas in your life you need to deal with, by using the excuse that your wretched looks are the reason you cannot do so?

If you really do want to make changes, then we suggest that you set achievable goals and work towards them. You can use a chart such as the one below to record these.

Appearance changes I would like to make

Physical characteristic I need to feel better about (e.g. flabby body):
What I need to do to improve this particular physical characteristic (e.g. firm up my physique and lose some weight):
Now break this down into tiny, achievable steps (e.g. find out about gym costs/locality; make a decision to join; see a trainer about my problems and work out a programme; ask for some dietary advice to accompany the physical workout; set a time limit for achieving my goal; set a start date):
Performance record/how am I doing? (e.g. week 1 achievements; week 2 achievements; work within whatever goal plan time frame you have set):

Using this chart will help you to work out what changes you would like to make, and how you could make them. This is a proactive approach that should result in a 'feel-good' factor from both the effort and positive results. Simply making the decision to work on these things should prove motivational and inspirational.

Low self-esteem can lead to 'not bothering' with ourselves. So, make an effort to do all you can to improve your physical appearance.

Give this a go. If you feel no better at all, you know at least that your problems lie in other perhaps unexplored areas and you should return to some of the earlier parts of this book.

self-esteem
and
relationships

A major area of our lives that can be affected by our low self-esteem is that of relationships. We may feel friendless and/or we may have difficulty in finding or holding on to romantic love. At the bottom of these difficulties lie our own feelings of inadequacy: 'I am not especially lovable/likable, so why would anyone really care about me?'

As we'll discover in this chapter, the problem is that with low esteem we tend to approach relationships from completely the wrong direction. We hope to find in the relationship all the feelings of self-worth and self-respect that we lack, rather than nurturing them in and for ourselves and bringing them *to* the relationship. It's not hard to see, then, how low self-esteem can be a recipe for relationship disaster – to your partner you will seem needy and vulnerable and he or she will feel under pressure.

In this chapter, please remember that we're not attempting to simplify the many complex problems that exist in relationships, but are focusing solely on issues of self-esteem.

Do you have a self-esteem problem with relationships?

Answer the questions below, and tick any that apply to you.

1 Are you in a relationship that you worry about?
2 Would you like to be in a relationship, but feel that you don't have enough to offer?
3 Do you accept sub-standard relationships because you feel you are not worth a good one?
4 Are you waiting for your partner to 'find you out' and see that you are really not worth loving?
5 Do you tend to 'hold back' in relationships so that your partner does not discover all your faults and weakness?
6 Do you actively avoid relationships because you cannot conceive of yourself as lovable?
7 Do you tend to sabotage good relationships on the basis that it will all end in tears at some point?
8 Do you spoil relationships by being very needy?
9 Do you pick arguments simply to rouse your partner to show that he or she 'really cares'?
10 Do you feel you will ever feel really loved and content?

Unfortunately, if you ticked even one of these statements, your self-esteem is sabotaging your relationship chances. Confidence in relationships comes only from confidence in ourselves. We need to learn to like ourselves first.

How to gain confidence in your relationship

Many people say that they have difficulty finding a relationship. This can be because we expect too much of other people – especially if we need them to enhance our self-esteem.

To increase your self-esteem, you need to adjust your thinking and practise changing your behaviour. Begin by taking a real interest in the people you meet.

This is an excellent skill for self-esteem. Building on the work in the last section, you are basically 'off-focusing'. Instead of thinking about *yourself*, *your* needs, *your* inadequacies, you focus on who you are with and ensure you find out about them.

Good communication

When we communicate well with friends or partners, we feel confident and good about ourselves. Poor communication can make us angry and upset, or fuels feelings of inadequacy.

In your closest relationships this means listening well. When we are in very intimate relationships we spend a great deal of time either talking or waiting for our partner to finish speaking so that we can say our next piece. We don't actively listen.

Understanding

Communicating well with your partner will give you confidence. You will communicate well if you first listen to what they have to say and then ensuring that you have understood it by commenting in a constructive way.

For example, if James tells Mary that he is unhappy that she doesn't like him spending time in the pub with his friends, she will do better not to respond with a statement, such as: 'You obviously prefer being there rather than here with me.' A better response would be to understand what he is saying and express how she feels, so that he is given the opportunity to find a solution. For example: 'I appreciate that you like to be able to relax after work with your friends sometimes, but I miss you as well. How can we resolve this?'

Exercise

With everyone you come into contact with today, either at work, at home or socially, speak less and listen more. Be aware of the outcomes.

How do you feel about yourself and what is your perception of how others view you when you do this?

An easy trick – just be nice!

How simple is that?! Let's explain it this way... One of the difficulties in relationships is our high expectations. The lower our self-esteem, the higher our expectations are. We 'need' our partner to do all the right things:

* to notice if we're unhappy
* to buy the right birthday present
* to spot our new haircut or the weight we have lost
* we need *them* to make *us* feel good about ourselves.

The result of these demands can be disappointment, and this will confirm our worst fears; we have either made a bad choice of partner or we are not worth treating lovingly and well.

Where is the focus here? Yes, we're back chasing our self-esteem again. Looking to achieve good self-esteem from our partner in our relationship, failing to find it, becoming distressed, feeling worse. We have again become totally self-focused. It's all about US again.

You may say that you have a tricky partner – who does not deserve warmth and kindness – and will take you for granted if you do. Unfortunately, it is not in the remit of this book to deal with difficult relationships, and you may have to make your own decisions here. We are attempting to help you find ways to increase your own self-esteem within your relationship – *even if this eventually encourages you to have the confidence to leave a relationship that is unrewarding*.

Using openness and honesty

When our self-esteem is low, it is easy to sabotage relationships with defeatist behaviour. This can include assuming the worst, focusing on the negative, not appearing vulnerable – the type of behaviour that means your partner never really gets to know the real person.

To succeed in dislodging low self-esteem associated with any area of your life, you need to take a risk. You can:

* stretch yourself a little
* change defeatist behaviours
* do something new without being certain of the outcome.

It is no different with intimate relationships. A saying worth remembering is: 'To risk nothing, is to risk everything.' Yes, you might get hurt if a relationship goes wrong – but you can learn to cope, and can save your energies to deal with that if it happens. Don't waste your energies on it now. You can risk:

* being open
* speaking from your heart
* letting your partner know the *real* you.

Exercise

Each day this week, tell someone close to you one aspect about yourself that they did not know before. Note how easy or difficult you found that, and any notable response from the other person. Make openness part of your daily life.

Surviving a break-up with your self-esteem intact

When a relationship ends – and not of our choosing – it can have the most devastating effect on our self-esteem, if we allow it. The pain of losing someone we love can be heartbreaking and any extra pain caused by thinking we are worthless and unlovable can be extremely hard to bear. It's no wonder we may feel depressed. In some cases, people repeat this. They see the ending as a sign that they are not worthy of being loved and that this is how things would undoubtedly end on another occasion.

While accepting heartbreak, you don't have to allow your self-worth to be called into question.

Use your thinking skills

One of the most important skills is not to generalize the specific. This particular relationship did not work out. This particular person turned out not to be right for you. This does not mean you are unlovable. Use your evidence-finding skills and ask yourself these questions:

* Have you ever been loved before?
* Who else has loved you in your life?
* What does this mean about your lovability?

Behave with dignity

Remember, you have choices. You could do the following:

* Don't say too much. It's easy to pour out invective, go into detail about how you feel, what happened when and so on. Say as little as possible and you will be respected for this, and (most importantly) you will respect yourself.
* If you still love the person, tell them so, but with grace and dignity and without asking anything in return.
* Determine not to contact them or behave in any way that you may regret later.
* Be certain that, however your heart is breaking, you have done nothing wrong and should hold your head up high. The difference this type of dignity will make to your self-esteem in the aftermath will be quite spectacular.

You cannot always keep the person you loved, but you can keep your self-esteem if you act with dignity.

Exercise

If you have found yourself in this situation in the past, look back at how you dealt with it. What lowered your self-esteem the most?

If it was to do with your own behaviour, what could you learn from that?

Intimate relationships can invoke the highest of emotions. In turn, high emotion can overturn rational behaviour; we can find ourselves failing to manage our emotions at all, but rather letting them manage us. If you are in a relationship where you lack confidence do please reread this chapter, and then put into practice what you have learned. The difference in your self-esteem – and consequently the quality of your relationships – will surprise you.